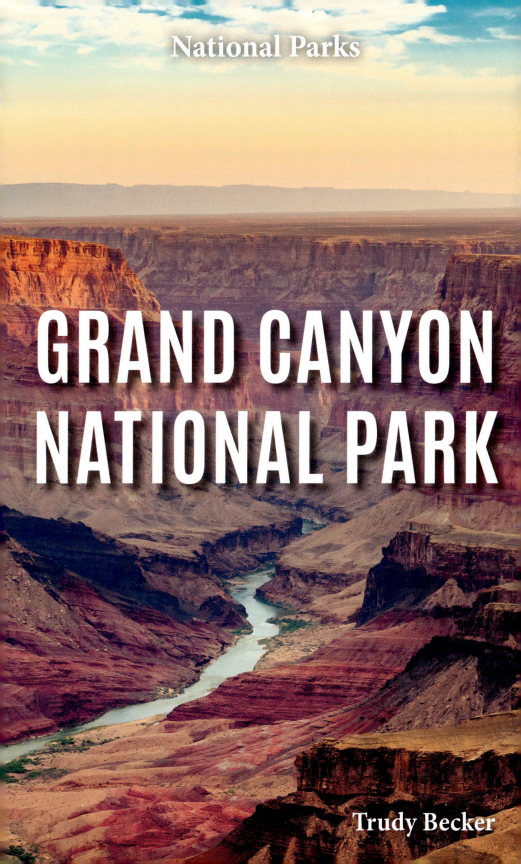

National Parks

GRAND CANYON NATIONAL PARK

Trudy Becker

WWW.APEXEDITIONS.COM

Copyright © 2025 by Apex Editions, Mendota Heights, MN 55120. All rights reserved. No part of this book may be reproduced or utilized in any form or by any means without written permission from the publisher.

Apex is distributed by North Star Editions:
sales@northstareditions.com | 888-417-0195

Produced for Apex by Red Line Editorial.

Photographs ©: Shutterstock Images, cover, 1, 4–5, 8–9, 10–11, 12–13, 14–15, 16–17, 18–19, 24–25, 30–31, 34–35, 36–37, 39, 40–41, 42–43, 44–45, 46–47, 48–49, 50–51, 52–53, 56–57; iStockphoto, 6–7, 29; Charles Phelps Cushing/ClassicStock/Archive Photos/Getty Images, 20–21; Corbis Historical/Getty Images, 22–23; Felicia Fonseca/AP Images, 26–27; Red Line Editorial, 32–33, 59; Travis Francis/US Fish and Wildlife Service/AP Images, 54–55; National Park Service, 58–59

Library of Congress Control Number: 2024943995

ISBN
979-8-89250-454-6 (hardcover)
979-8-89250-470-6 (paperback)
979-8-89250-501-7 (ebook pdf)
979-8-89250-486-7 (hosted ebook)

Printed in the United States of America
Mankato, MN
012025

NOTE TO PARENTS AND EDUCATORS

Apex books are designed to build literacy skills in striving readers. Exciting, high-interest content attracts and holds readers' attention. The text is carefully leveled to allow students to achieve success quickly.

TABLE OF CONTENTS

Chapter 1
HIKE TO MATHER POINT 5

Chapter 2
ALL ABOUT THE GRAND CANYON 8

Chapter 3
PEOPLE AND THE CANYON 18

Natural Wonder
DEER CREEK FALLS 28

Chapter 4
FUN AT THE CANYON 31

Natural Wonder
PIPE CREEK VISTA 38

Chapter 5
WILDLIFE 40

Chapter 6
SAVING THE PARK 50

PARK MAP • 58
COMPREHENSION QUESTIONS • 60
GLOSSARY • 62
TO LEARN MORE • 63
ABOUT THE AUTHOR • 63
INDEX • 64

On a clear day, visitors can see for more than 30 miles (48 km) from Mather Point.

HIKE TO MATHER POINT

Two hikers enter Grand Canyon National Park. They set out on a path. The hikers move through the desert habitat. They spot lizards and birds. Soon, they reach Mather Point.

The hikers gasp at the sight. In front of them, an enormous canyon stretches 10 miles (16 km) across. Then the hikers look down. The bottom is 1 mile (1.6 km) below them. The hikers feel goosebumps.

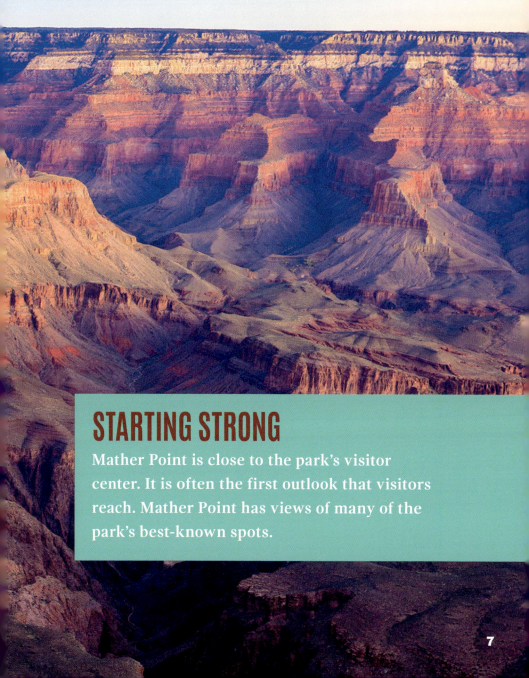

Sunrise is a popular time to visit Mather Point.

STARTING STRONG

Mather Point is close to the park's visitor center. It is often the first outlook that visitors reach. Mather Point has views of many of the park's best-known spots.

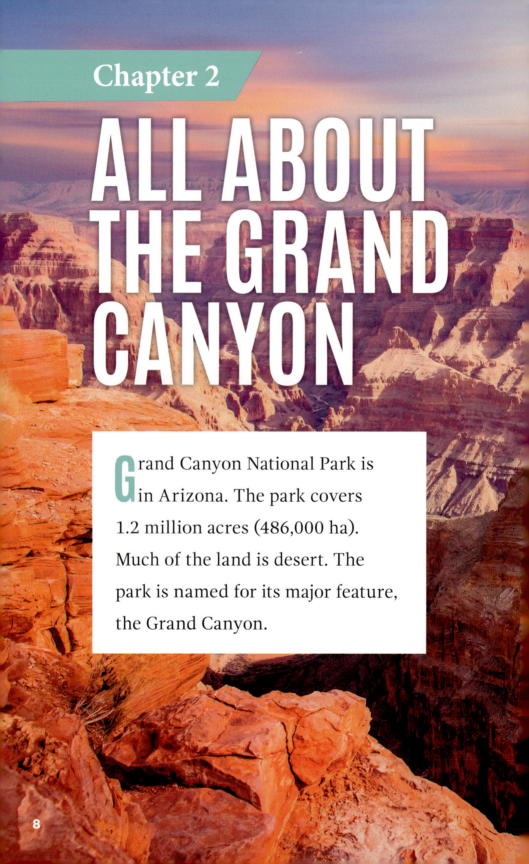

Chapter 2

ALL ABOUT THE GRAND CANYON

Grand Canyon National Park is in Arizona. The park covers 1.2 million acres (486,000 ha). Much of the land is desert. The park is named for its major feature, the Grand Canyon.

The Grand Canyon is one of the largest canyons on Earth.

The Grand Canyon is massive. It stretches for 277 miles (446 km). At its widest point, the canyon is 18 miles (29 km) across. Its deepest point is 6,000 feet (1,829 m) from the top. The canyon formed millions of years ago. Over time, moving water carved out the rock.

FROM THE PAST

People have found lots of fossils in the Grand Canyon. The fossils show what animals used to live there. Many fossils are of small sea creatures.

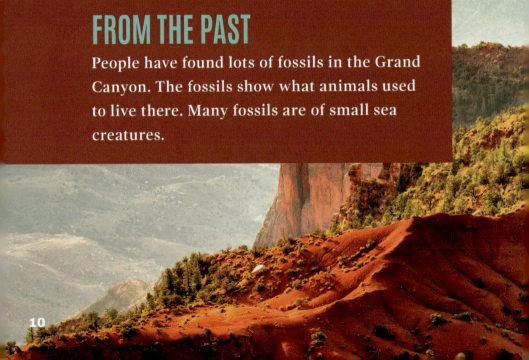

The North Rim of the canyon is usually cooler than the South Rim.

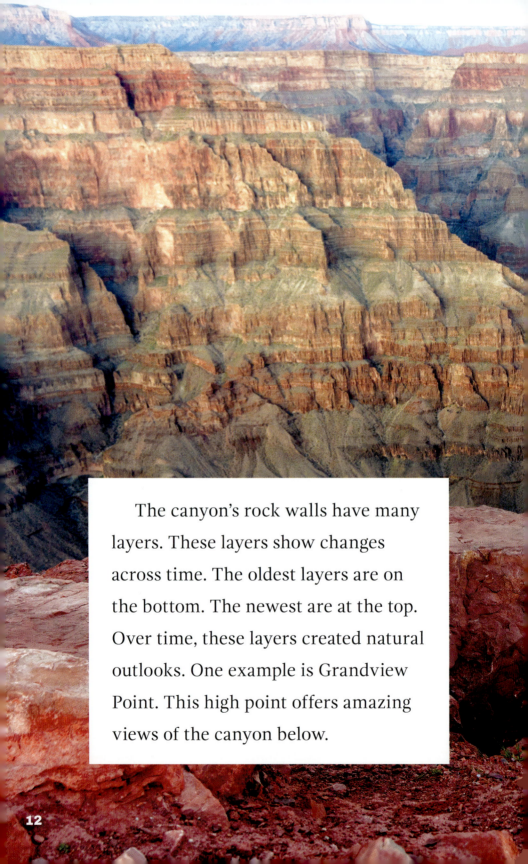

The canyon's rock walls have many layers. These layers show changes across time. The oldest layers are on the bottom. The newest are at the top. Over time, these layers created natural outlooks. One example is Grandview Point. This high point offers amazing views of the canyon below.

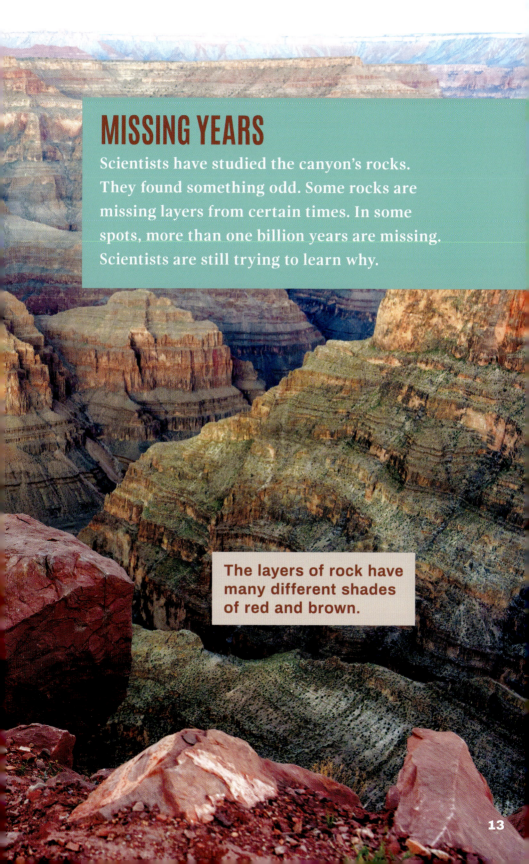

MISSING YEARS

Scientists have studied the canyon's rocks. They found something odd. Some rocks are missing layers from certain times. In some spots, more than one billion years are missing. Scientists are still trying to learn why.

The layers of rock have many different shades of red and brown.

The Colorado River runs along the bottom of the canyon. This river travels 277 miles (446 km) through the canyon. But the river flows much longer. It stretches more than 1,500 miles (2,400 km) in total. The river helps wildlife and humans survive in the area. It is a key part of the ecosystem.

WATER PROBLEMS

The Colorado River is a water source for many people. However, humans have used too much of the river's water. Also, climate change is making the area drier. As a result, the river is in danger. It has much less water than it did in the past. That has harmed many plants and animals.

The Colorado River runs from the Rocky Mountains to the Pacific Ocean.

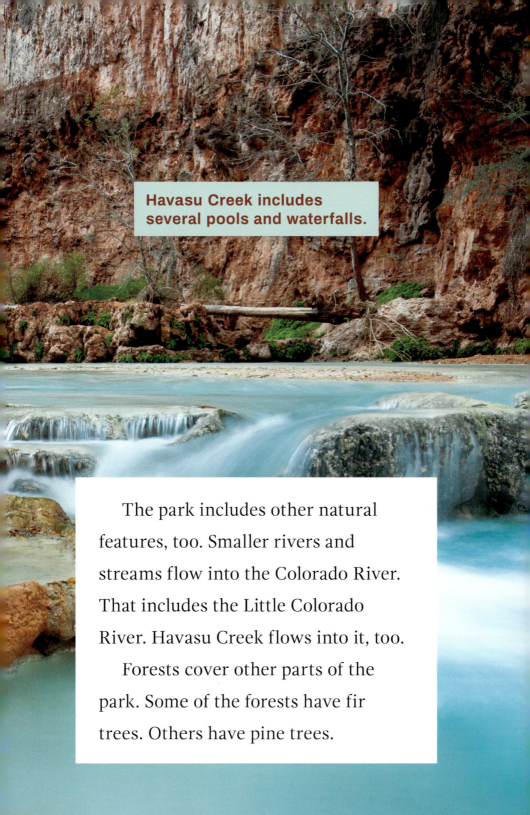

Havasu Creek includes several pools and waterfalls.

The park includes other natural features, too. Smaller rivers and streams flow into the Colorado River. That includes the Little Colorado River. Havasu Creek flows into it, too.

Forests cover other parts of the park. Some of the forests have fir trees. Others have pine trees.

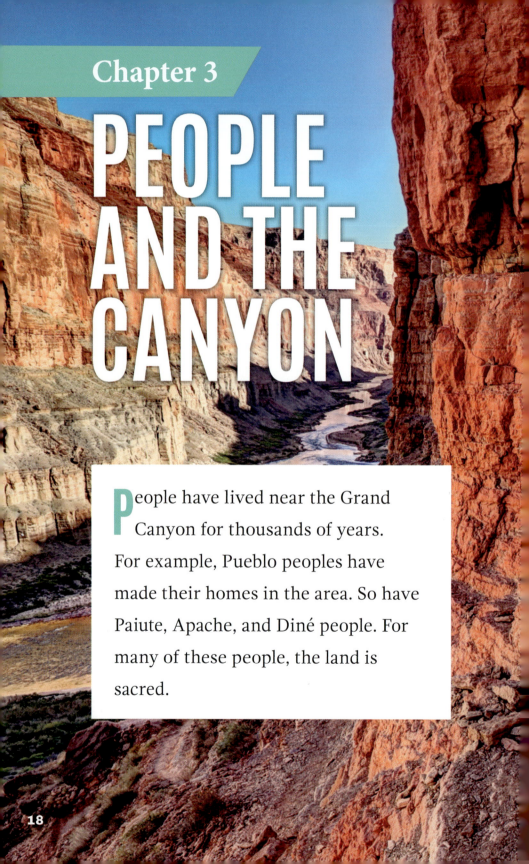

Chapter 3

PEOPLE AND THE CANYON

People have lived near the Grand Canyon for thousands of years. For example, Pueblo peoples have made their homes in the area. So have Paiute, Apache, and Diné people. For many of these people, the land is sacred.

Ancient people built rooms into the wall of the canyon. They stored food in these rooms.

The Havasupai used the land for centuries. They hunted large animals. They farmed corn, pumpkins, and other crops. But by 1540, European explorers had reached the area. Over time, they pushed most Indigenous people out. In the late 1800s, the US government fought the Havasupai. The United States took even more land.

HAVASUPAI LAND

Some Havasupai people still live in the Grand Canyon. They live on a reservation. It borders the national park. The area includes the beautiful Havasu Falls.

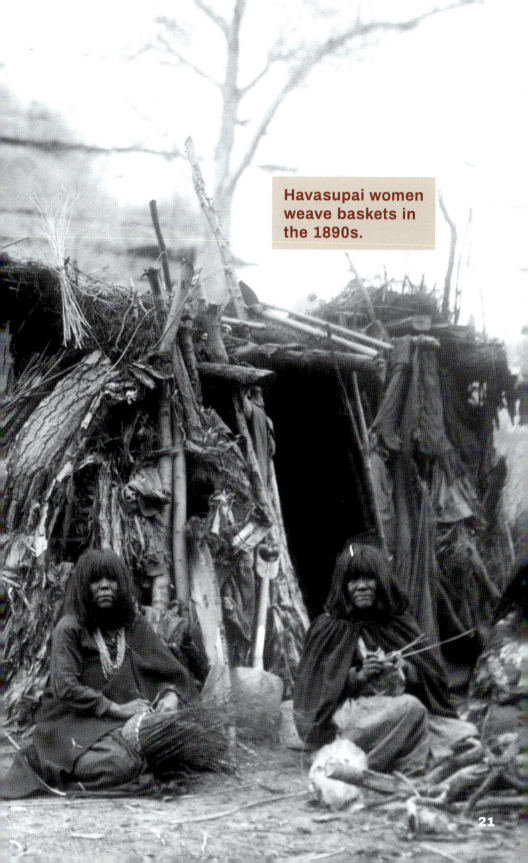

Havasupai women weave baskets in the 1890s.

Other changes happened in the 1800s. Stories of gold reached the eastern United States. So, people came to the canyon hoping to get rich. Tourism grew as well. Visitors came to see the beautiful sights. The area already had trails. But workers built new trails for the visitors. Some are still used today.

In the 1870s, the US government sent people to explore the area.

23

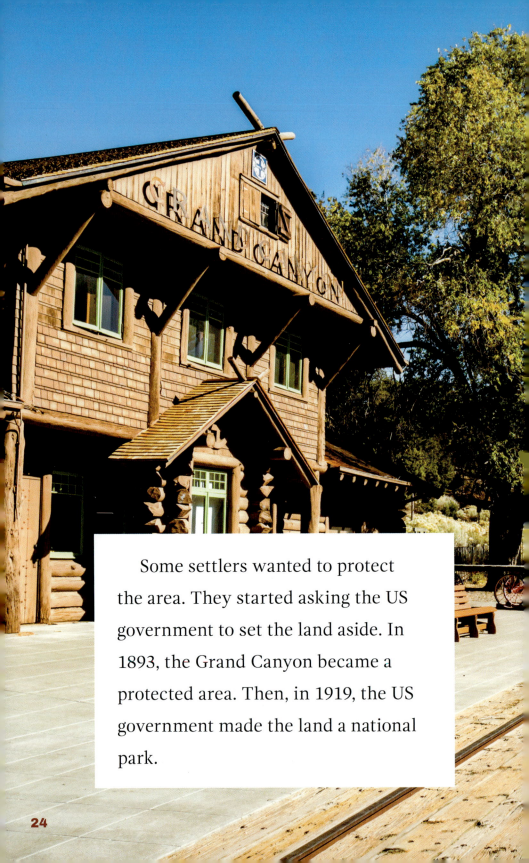

Some settlers wanted to protect the area. They started asking the US government to set the land aside. In 1893, the Grand Canyon became a protected area. Then, in 1919, the US government made the land a national park.

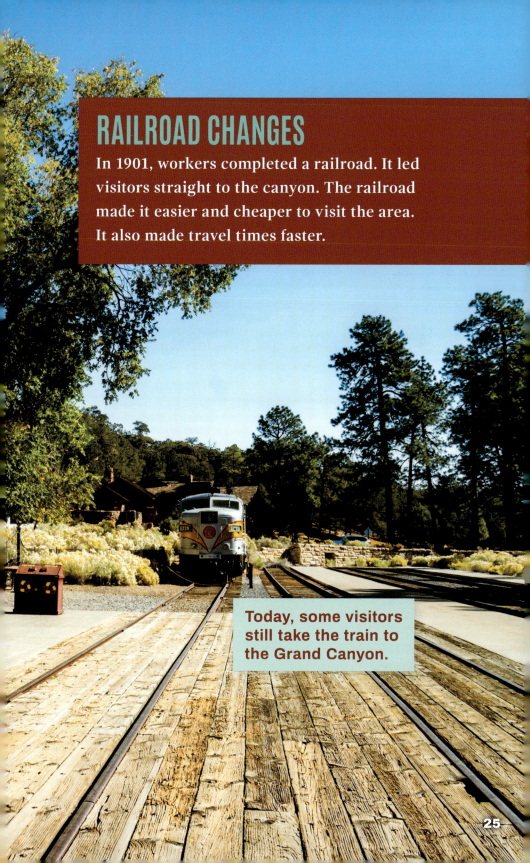

RAILROAD CHANGES

In 1901, workers completed a railroad. It led visitors straight to the canyon. The railroad made it easier and cheaper to visit the area. It also made travel times faster.

Today, some visitors still take the train to the Grand Canyon.

In 2023, the park renamed one of its campgrounds to honor the Havasupai people.

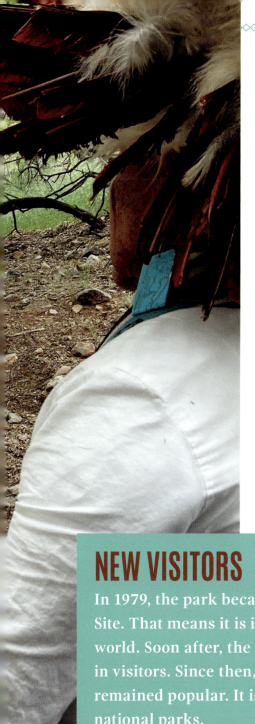

In the 1900s, people developed the park. They built the Grand Canyon Lodge. They updated old trails. They also built new ones. Later, workers added welcome buildings and information sites. By the 2020s, the park received nearly five million visitors each year.

NEW VISITORS

In 1979, the park became a World Heritage Site. That means it is important to the whole world. Soon after, the area got a huge boost in visitors. Since then, the Grand Canyon has remained popular. It is one of the most visited national parks.

Natural Wonder

DEER CREEK FALLS

Deer Creek Falls is a famous waterfall in the park. Deer Creek winds through a rocky canyon until it reaches the falls. Then the creek plunges over a cliff. The water falls more than 100 feet (30 m). It enters the Colorado River down below.

Visitors can see the falls in two ways. Some people reach the spot by hiking. But most visitors arrive by raft. The falls is a short walk from the Colorado River.

Deer Creek Falls is a difficult 9-mile (14-km) hike from the top of the Grand Canyon.

Rafting is a popular activity at the Grand Canyon.

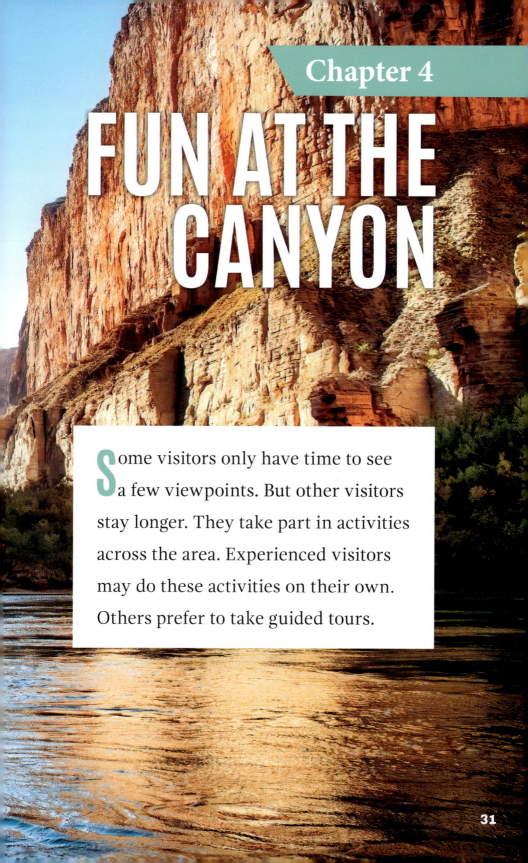

Chapter 4

FUN AT THE CANYON

Some visitors only have time to see a few viewpoints. But other visitors stay longer. They take part in activities across the area. Experienced visitors may do these activities on their own. Others prefer to take guided tours.

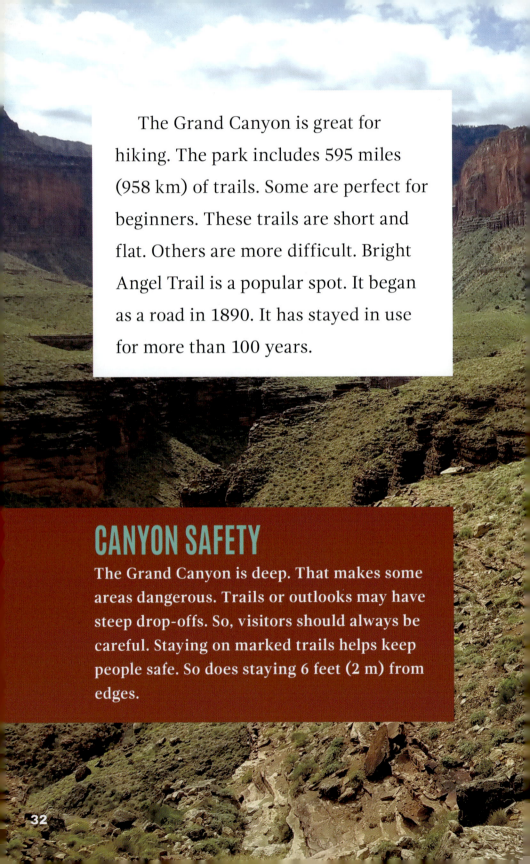

The Grand Canyon is great for hiking. The park includes 595 miles (958 km) of trails. Some are perfect for beginners. These trails are short and flat. Others are more difficult. Bright Angel Trail is a popular spot. It began as a road in 1890. It has stayed in use for more than 100 years.

CANYON SAFETY

The Grand Canyon is deep. That makes some areas dangerous. Trails or outlooks may have steep drop-offs. So, visitors should always be careful. Staying on marked trails helps keep people safe. So does staying 6 feet (2 m) from edges.

Some trails go all the way down to the bottom of the canyon.

Mules are sure-footed on narrow trails.

Summer is a popular time to visit the park. The Colorado River offers many options in warm weather. Visitors can go whitewater rafting. They can also ride other kinds of boats. Dories are light and fast. These boats can blast through the rapids.

MULE TRIPS

Visitors can move through the park in many ways. Hiking and boating are the most popular. But some visitors take mule rides. Guides lead the animals along the trails.

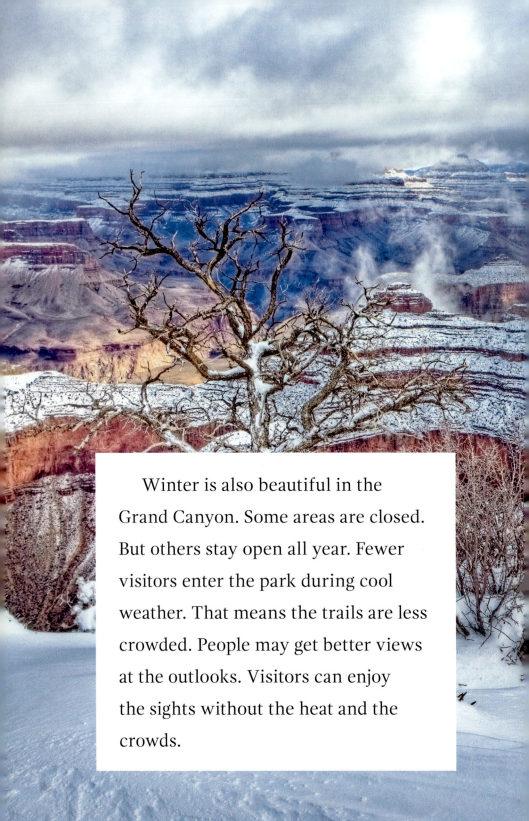

Winter is also beautiful in the Grand Canyon. Some areas are closed. But others stay open all year. Fewer visitors enter the park during cool weather. That means the trails are less crowded. People may get better views at the outlooks. Visitors can enjoy the sights without the heat and the crowds.

During winter, snow covers the upper parts of the canyon.

WHERE TO STAY

The park offers a variety of places to spend the night. There are several lodges. Some rooms have excellent views of the canyon. The park also has 13 campgrounds. And there are many hotels outside the park.

Natural Wonder

PIPE CREEK VISTA

Pipe Creek Vista is one of the canyon's best vistas. Visitors can reach it by car or bike. They can also arrive on foot.

The outlook offers views of different areas of the park. Visitors can look out across the canyon. They can spot Mather Point. They can also see Yaki Point.

Pipe Creek Vista is a great place for bird-watching. Several kinds of birds fly through the area. Visitors can also spot a beautiful forest of Douglas fir trees.

Pipe Creek Vista is on the South Rim of the Grand Canyon.

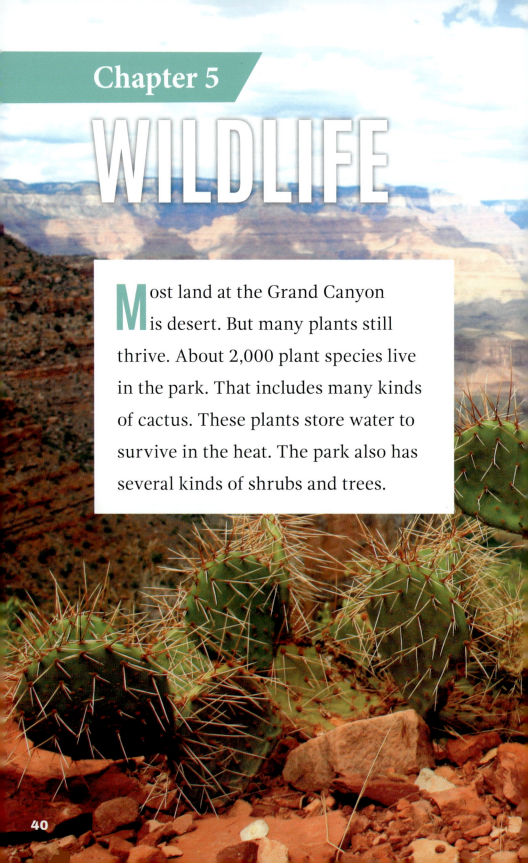

Chapter 5

WILDLIFE

Most land at the Grand Canyon is desert. But many plants still thrive. About 2,000 plant species live in the park. That includes many kinds of cactus. These plants store water to survive in the heat. The park also has several kinds of shrubs and trees.

The prickly pear cactus is a common sight at the Grand Canyon.

Birds are some of the most common animals in the park. There are more than 400 different kinds. Some live by the canyon all through the year. Others stop briefly as they migrate. Rare birds, such as the California condor, live there. So do raptors. Near the water, beautiful river birds can be seen. These include herons and kingfishers.

The California condor has a wingspan of 9.5 feet (2.9 m).

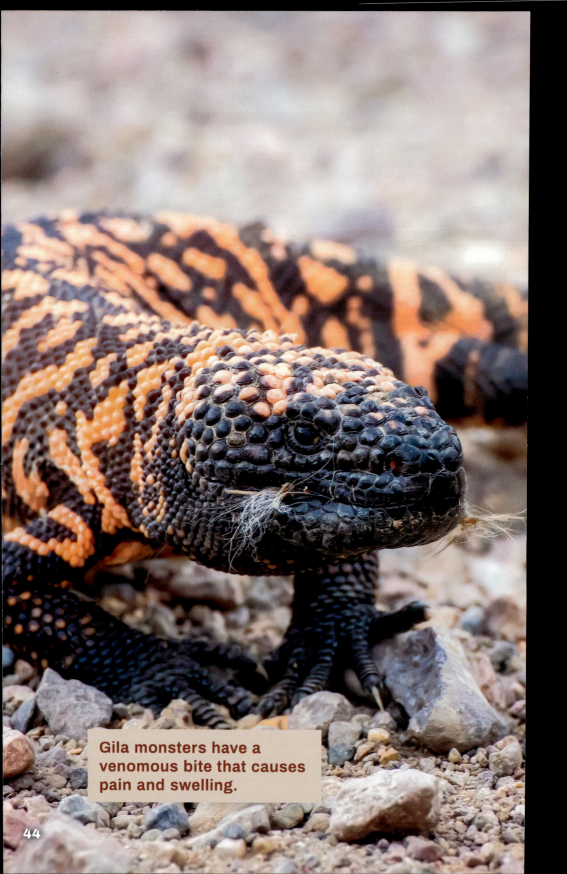
Gila monsters have a venomous bite that causes pain and swelling.

Snakes, lizards, and tortoises are common reptiles in the park. Reptiles do not make their own body heat. So, hot deserts are great places for them. Short-horned lizards blend into the brown ground. They stay still and then rush out to catch food. Rattlesnakes live in the Grand Canyon, too. They are the park's most venomous animal.

GILA MONSTERS

Gila monsters are the biggest reptiles in the park. During summer months, they sleep during the day. They hunt at dusk and dawn. Gila monsters use their tongues to sniff out prey. Then they attack.

Many mammals live in the park, too. The biggest are bison and elk. Visitors sometimes spot them near roads and trails. Mountain lions also roam the park. So do ringtails. These small animals have big eyes and ears.

The ringtail is a member of the raccoon family. It is the state mammal of Arizona.

BATS ALL AROUND

The Grand Canyon is full of bats. It has more kinds of bats than almost any other place in the United States. The little brown bat is a common type. One of these bats can eat 1,200 insects in an hour.

Insects and arachnids are key parts of the Grand Canyon's wildlife. Bark scorpions live by streams. Tarantulas live all across the park. The largest tarantulas stay down in the canyon. Hundreds of kinds of butterflies live in the park, too.

TREE FROGS

Canyon tree frogs are a common frog in the park. These small frogs are just 2 inches (5 cm) long. The frogs avoid dry areas. Instead, they stay close to streams.

The Grand Canyon black tarantula can grow to 4 inches (10 cm) across.

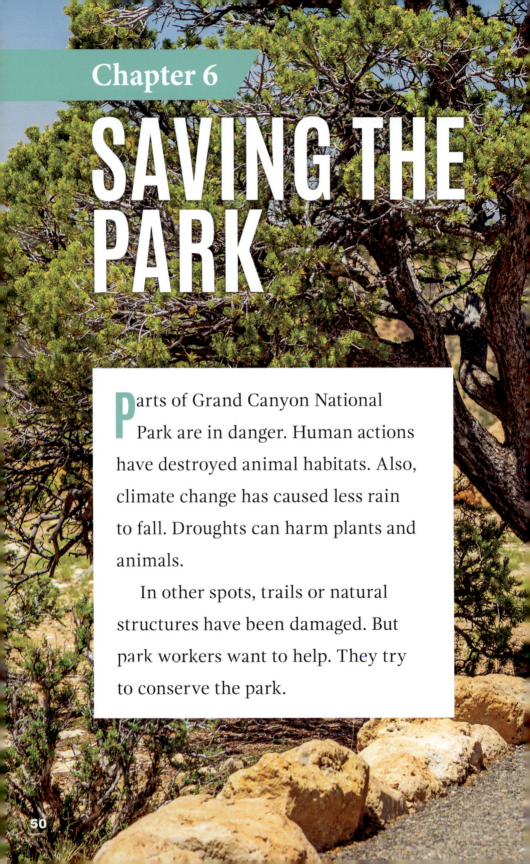

Chapter 6

SAVING THE PARK

Parts of Grand Canyon National Park are in danger. Human actions have destroyed animal habitats. Also, climate change has caused less rain to fall. Droughts can harm plants and animals.

In other spots, trails or natural structures have been damaged. But park workers want to help. They try to conserve the park.

Hundreds of people work at Grand Canyon National Park.

Some projects help increase animal populations. For example, the park is home to a fish called the humpback chub. Scientists took out some other fish that threatened the chub. It worked. The chub's numbers grew. In other cases, big populations can be dangerous. For instance, park workers have removed some bison.

SPECIAL PLANTS

The sentry milk vetch grows in the Grand Canyon. This plant is not found anywhere else on Earth. In the 1990s, workers began to fence the plant in. They wanted to keep people and animals out.

Park workers have moved many bison onto the lands of nearby Indigenous people.

Some projects focus on entire ecosystems. Park workers try to keep invasive species out. For example, they check boats that enter the park. That way, they can stop invasive fish from reaching the waters. Scientists also try to save plants. They keep non-native seeds out. These projects keep the areas balanced.

FOLLOW THE COLOR
Wildlife rely on the area's water. But hotter temperatures are making the park drier. So, scientists study the water's quality. They also find out how it flows. They use colored dye to do this. They can see the water's path.

The humpback chub is one type of native fish that scientists are trying to protect.

55

Ribbon Falls is an 8-mile (13-km) hike from the North Rim of the Grand Canyon.

Weather wears down the park's trails. Hiking does, too. So, some areas start to erode. Park workers fix and rebuild them. One project was for a new Ribbon Falls Bridge. Projects such as this one help keep visitors safe. They help protect the park's land and wildlife, too.

PARK MAP

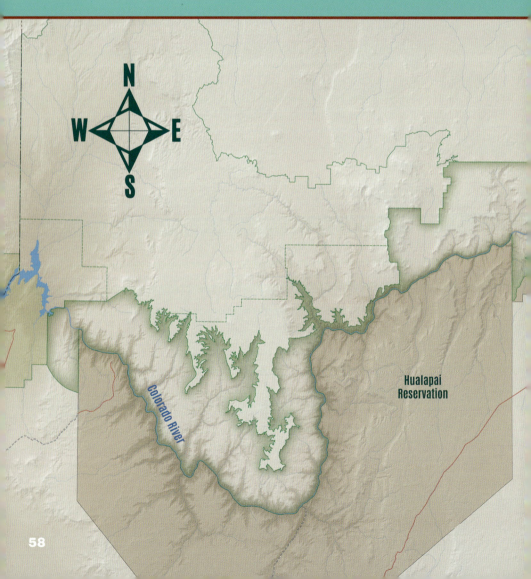

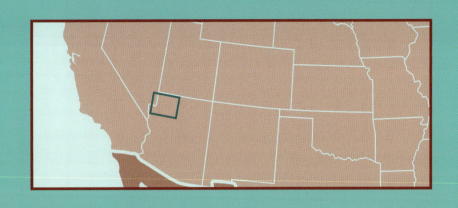
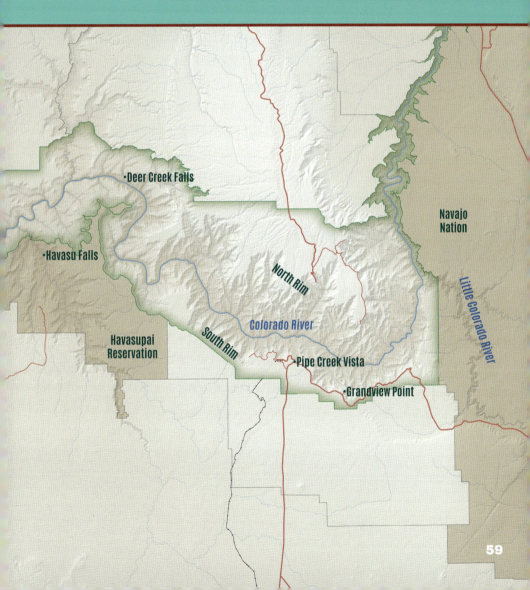

COMPREHENSION QUESTIONS

Write your answers on a separate piece of paper.

1. Write a few sentences describing different things visitors can do in Grand Canyon National Park.

2. If you visited the Grand Canyon, what would you be most excited to see? Why?

3. What is the most venomous animal in the Grand Canyon?

   A. rattlesnake

   B. little brown bat

   C. canyon tree frog

4. How do visitors erode trails?

   A. Visitors always stay in their cars.

   B. Many visitors walk on the same trail.

   C. Visitors usually create new trails.

5. What does **migrate** mean in this book?

*Some live by the canyon all through the year. Others stop briefly as they **migrate**.*

    A. move to a new area

    B. drink water from a river

    C. stay somewhere forever

6. What does **droughts** mean in this book?

*Also, climate change has caused less rain to fall. **Droughts** can harm plants and animals.*

    A. times when there is too much rain

    B. times when there is not enough rain

    C. times when wildlife is safe from rain

Answer key on page 64.

GLOSSARY

canyon
A deep area that has steep sides.

climate change
A dangerous long-term change in Earth's temperature and weather patterns.

conserve
To save something from harm.

ecosystem
A group of living things and their environment.

erode
To wear away.

fossils
Remains of plants and animals that lived long ago.

invasive
Spreading quickly in a new area and causing many problems there.

lodge
A place where visitors can stay.

mammals
Animals that have hair and produce milk for their young.

rapids
Fast-flowing parts of a river.

venomous
Having a harmful substance that can be used to bite or sting prey.

TO LEARN MORE
BOOKS

Amstutz, Lisa J. *Canyons*. North Mankato, MN: Capstone Press, 2021.

London, Martha. *Grand Canyon*. Minneapolis: Abdo Publishing, 2021.

Tieck, Sarah. *Arizona*. Minneapolis: Abdo Publishing, 2020.

ONLINE RESOURCES

Visit **www.apexeditions.com** to find links and resources related to this title.

ABOUT THE AUTHOR

Trudy Becker lives in Minneapolis, Minnesota. She likes exploring new places and loves anything involving books.

INDEX

arachnids, 48

bats, 47
birds, 5, 38, 42
bison, 46, 52
Bright Angel Trail, 32

camping, 37
climate change, 14, 50
Colorado River, 14, 17, 28, 35
conservation, 50, 52, 54, 57

Deer Creek Falls, 28

elk, 46

forests, 17, 38
fossils, 10

Gila monsters, 45
Grandview Point, 12

Havasu Falls, 20
Havasupai people, 20
hiking, 5–6, 28, 32, 35, 57

Indigenous people, 18, 20
insects, 47–48

layers, 12–13
lizards, 5, 45
lodges, 27, 37

Mather Point, 5, 7, 38
mule rides, 35

Pipe Creek Vista, 38

rafting, 28, 35
railroad, 25
ringtails, 46

snakes, 45

trails, 22, 27, 32, 35–36, 46, 50, 57

waterfalls, 28

ANSWER KEY:

1. Answers will vary; 2. Answers will vary; 3. A; 4. B; 5. A; 6. B